The Anti-Semitic Subtext of "American Carnage"

-By Laurel Federbush

A lot of people did some speculating about what Trump may have meant by the line in his acceptance speech about "American carnage." People ridiculed it for being over-the-top, like something from death-metal music or a video game. Others commented on how dark it was, apocalyptic even. Maybe influenced by the European philosophers that Steve Bannon, who likely wrote the speech, often quotes.

That phrase just sort of stuck out like a sore thumb. What did it mean? What did our new president mean?

Maybe it doesn't seem so important now, in light of all the new developments with this strange presidency. Water under the bridge. Still, if we could discover the origins of that strange phrase, "American Carnage," it might help illuminate things, at least a little.

Here's a bit of the speech in question. This part is
from the beginning:

"For too long, a small group in our nation's capital
has reaped the rewards of government while the
people have borne the cost. Washington
flourished, but the people did not share in its
wealth. Politicians prospered, but the jobs left and
the factories closed. The establishment protected
itself, but not the citizens of our country. Their
victories have not been your victories. Their
triumphs have not been your triumphs. And while
they celebrated in our nation's capital, there was
little to celebrate for struggling families all across
our land."

Now let's skip ahead to the carnage part...

"But for too many of our citizens, a different
reality exists: mothers and children trapped in

poverty in our inner cities; rusted out factories scattered like tombstones across the landscape of our nation; an education system flush with cash, but which leaves our young and beautiful students deprived of all knowledge; and the crime and the gangs and the drugs that have stolen too many lives and robbed our country of so much unrealized potential.

This American carnage stops right here and stops right now."

American carnage.

Let me ask you a question: Are you someone who lies awake at night worrying about the future of the white race? No? Then you may not have a clue what Trump was talking about.

Perhaps you have heard about "white genocide"? Genocide—that's a horrendous thing. Innocent people being ruthlessly slaughtered by the millions. Bet you didn't realize that that was happening to white people...because it isn't.

Not that there may not be killings of some people in some places just because they're white, and that is certainly an unconscionable hate crime. But it isn't genocide. There is no wide-scale slaughter, no organized attempt to wipe white people off the face of the earth.

No, what is meant by "white genocide" is racial equality. Diversity. Multiculturalism. Welcoming in refugees who are fleeing persecution. By treating everyone equally, regardless of race, as our Constitution demands; by preserving a society where people of different races can peacefully coexist; the racists would have us believe that by doing these things, which are part of simple human decency, we are committing the genocide of white people. People who aren't white (including Jews) are supposedly committing "white genocide" just by existing.

Why? Because white people can't compete on a level playing field? Seems like the white supremacists would more accurately be called "white inferiorists," because they apparently have so little faith in their own race.

But continuing with their funny theory: it's about how the there's a conspiracy to destroy the white race and its superior culture through mass immigration of Muslims, Hispanics, and other examples of the "darker races." There would be interracial breeding, and lo and behold! The skin color of the next generation would no longer be white.

Now, among the many ridiculous things in this line of thinking, you may have noticed that they're acting as if there's such a thing as "white culture." There isn't. Whether there's even such a thing as race at all is even suspect. But there's certainly no such thing as a culture that revolves around a skin color. The Slavs and the Celts had very different cultures. But these racists aren't too keen on real history.

To bolster their arguments, they'll refer to the sinister "Coudenhove-Kalergi Plan," named after the founder of the European Union.

In order to appreciate just how sick these people are, you'd need to know who they're talking about. The Austrian-Japanese politician and philosopher Richard Nikolaus Eijiro, Count of Coudenhove-Kalergi (a.k.a. Richard von Coudenhove-Kalergi) did, in fact, want to create a Europe that was conducive to people of different races and ethnicities living together in harmony, instead of nations being divided along racial and ethnic lines. In the wake of World War I, he breathed the same Austrian air as Adoph Hitler did. But Coudenhove-Kalergi's guiding spirits took him in a completely different direction.

For forty-nine years he served as founding president of the Paneuropean Union, which eventually resulted in the European Union.

He was the real-life hero upon whom *Casablanca's* Victor Laszlo was based. While fleeing the Nazis from country to country, he continued to work tirelessly for his vision of a Europe united in peaceful coexistence and diversity.

And most of us would be on our knees begging to go back in a time machine, if we could, to entreat the post-WWI world to heed the words of the Count and turn away from that painter-turned-agitator…

But to the sickos of the white genocide crowd, this guy is an arch-villain. Not Hitler, but a man who risked his life to oppose Hitler and promote a better vision for the future.

By the way, Coudenhove-Kalergi proposed English
as the world language. Just thought I'd mention
that, in case you're envisioning him as the
destroyer of Western civilization today's white
supremacists would have you believe.

Here is one of his writings, from *Praktischer
Idealismus* (*Practical Idealism*), written in 1925,
that the white supremacists find particularly
galling:

"The man of the future will be of mixed race.
Today's races and classes will gradually disappear
owing to the vanishing of space, time, and
prejudice. The Eurasian-Negroid race of the
future, similar in its appearance to the Ancient
Egyptians, will replace the diversity of peoples
with a diversity of individuals. [...]

Instead of destroying European Jewry, Europe,
against its own will, refined and educated this
people into a future leader-nation through this
artificial selection process. No wonder that this
people, that escaped Ghetto-Prison, developed
into a spiritual nobility of Europe. Therefore a
gracious Providence provided Europe with a new

race of nobility by the Grace of Spirit. This happened at the moment when Europe's feudal aristocracy became dilapidated, and thanks to Jewish emancipation."

This statement of defiance against those intent on committing an actual genocide is how the racists support their contention that the white (sometimes called "Aryan") race is the victim in all of this.

As I mentioned, these white racialists don't consider Jews part of the white race. And some of them don't even consider Jews part of the human race. They think Jews are an alien race of reptilians. –Stop laughing! They're serious.

 So when Trump, Bannon et al. sabotage the European Union and promote ethnic nationalism, what they really mean is that they want to go back to the good old days of Hitler. It's that simple.

Under President Obama, the white racialists had a campaign of continually posting petitions to "Stop White Genocide" on the White House website. Interestingly, these petitions have met with more resistance to their posting under the Trump administration, likely because of the administration's aversion to all petitions rather than because of the specific content of this one.

But the slogan "Stop White Genocide" did get around, appearing on t-shirts, a Nazi website, and YouTube videos. There was even an incident where faculty and students at Harvard University found themselves subjected to "Stop White Genocide" e-mails from an unknown source (which is actually whitegenocideproject.com, as I discovered from that website).

"Stop White Genocide"... "This American carnage stops right here and stops right now." See any resemblance?

Now, I'm not the first person to suggest that Trump was talking about white genocide. But I want to develop that a bit, because there's more to say about it. Simply saying that Trump was referring to white genocide and leaving it at that isn't all there is with regard to the matter.

"White Genocide," sometimes called the "War on Whites," is often mentioned as a subtle thing, a way that whites are marginalized, pushed aside to make room for immigrants, in danger of extinction through breeding with other races...aren't these racists charming people?

But it isn't always talked about in terms of actual, literal violence.

Let's get back to Trump's speech.

By bringing up the idea of "carnage," Trump's speechwriter meant to point fingers at one specific ethnic group.

Although blacks and Hispanics were partly implicated in this via the association with inner-city violence, they are not the villains in this scenario, since the picture was painted of a mother trapped in poverty. So that inner-city mother, not necessarily black or Hispanic but likely so, is a victim, just like Trump's intended audience.

War and carnage…What group has been accused, throughout history, of profiting from war and carnage? Can't remember?

Here's a hint:

<u>The Jew of Malta</u> (notice that word "Jew" in the title), a 16th-century play by Christopher Marlowe,

has as its main character the anti-hero Barabas, a treacherous Jew who plots unsuccessfully to destroy his enemies with gunpowder. He gets his just deserts at the end, of course, as he burns to death in a cauldron.

Here's another hint:

" It is indispensable for our purpose that wars, so far as possible, should not result in territorial gains: war will thus be brought on to the economic ground, where the nations will not fail to perceive in the assistance we give the strength of our predominance, and this state of things will put both sides at the mercy of our international AGENTUR; which possesses millions of eyes ever on the watch and unhampered by any limitations whatsoever. Our international rights will then wipe out national rights, in the proper sense of right, and will rule the nations precisely as the civil law of States rules the relations of their subjects among themselves."

That's from "Economic Wars," or Protocol No. 2 from <u>The Protocols of the Learned Elders of Zion</u>, the infamous text purportedly exposing a Jewish plot for world dominance, exposed as a forgery by <u>The Times</u> of London in 1921.

Maybe this will jog your memory:

Today I will once more be a prophet: If the international Jewish financiers in and outside Europe should succeed in plunging the nations once more into a world war, then the result will not be the Bolshevization of the earth, and thus the victory of Jewry, but the annihilation of the Jewish race in Europe! ...The nations are no longer willing to die on the battlefield so that this unstable international race may profiteer from a war or satisfy its Old Testament vengeance. The Jewish watchword "Workers of the world unite" will be conquered by a higher realization, namely "Workers of all classes and of all nations, recognize your common enemy!"

That was from the speech to the *Reichstag*, or German parliament, given on January 30, 1939 by Adolph Hitler.

Or perhaps this will remind you:

"Jewish Copper Kings Reap Rich War-Profits."

That's the title of Chapter 27 of <u>The International Jew: The World's Foremost Problem</u>, by Henry Ford.

Or how about the 1942 reference by Ezra Pound to "the sixty kikes who started this war"? It's basically a summation of countless incoherent ravings by him on the subject.

And if that isn't enough, there are zillions of other places where you can find insinuations or outright declarations that Jews instigate wars in order to profit from them.

And, in fact, if you read the writings of those who are pushing the war-on-whites/white-genocide idea, they will specifically tell you that it's an evil design by the global-Zionist-Jewish elites to rule the world. Jews again profiting from a war, this time a war on whites.

So, to recap, we have war, the carnage of war, Jews profiting from the carnage, "American carnage"…

But why specify *American* carnage? As opposed to what—Swedish carnage? Why the need to say "American" when addressing an American audience? Certainly the world was watching, but at that point in his speech, Trump had been discussing America's domestic problems, so it hardly seems likely that he would need to throw in "American" just to be understood.

Wait a minute, there is one nationality that has been paired with the word "carnage."

If you're a history buff, you may have checked out Alistair Smith's book *Carnage: the German Front in World War One (Images of War)*. Full of rare photographs of what befell those hapless German troops and their villages.

So maybe the Trump speech specified *American* carnage to distinguish it from the carnage experienced by Germany in WWI. And to signal to certain people in the audience (admittedly a small group) that Trump and his cohorts hadn't forgotten what Germany had endured.

Or you might have come across *Bankers, Bradburys, Carnage and Slaughter* (1999),by Justin Walker. There's that word "carnage" again! This screed accuses Jewish bankers (the "House of Rothschild") of causing WWI, as well as the American Civil War.

But Trump's speech also referred to stopping the carnage. Remember? "This American carnage stops right here and it stops right now." Notice that the word "stops" occurs twice, so it must be important.

Come to think of it, there was a historical figure who "wished to stop the futile carnage," as an interviewer once said of him. Someone known throughout the world. Frequently referred to as a "hero," and a "martyr for peace." This person went on a courageous but ill-fated mission to try to stop an imminent war. He was captured and lived the rest of his life in prison.

Now, I'm not sure if Trump would want to be associated with that last part, since he famously likes people who weren't captured. But wanting to be associated with a courageous hero, a Christ-like martyr...he might just go along with that. And his speech would seem to assure us that he, unlike our sad hero, will succeed in stopping the carnage.

How happy for us that our president made a point of connecting himself with a man of such noble virtues.

The hero I refer to, of course, is Hitler's deputy, Rudolf Hess. A hero to the neo-Nazi movement, that is. His body has had to be exhumed to deter the swarms of neo-Nazis who would come to rally at his grave.

As Deputy Fuhrer, Hess had countless people executed or carted off to concentration camps. But that doesn't rate as "carnage" to a Nazi or a Nazi sympathizer.

The carnage that Hess sought to prevent was war between brothers of the Nordic race—the

Germans and the British. Also, he wanted to spare Germany from having to fight on two fronts.

So committed was he to this goal that he actually parachuted into Scotland, in hopes of somehow arranging a peace deal with the Duke of Hamilton. However, he was captured and spent the rest of his life in prison.

Hess didn't succeed in stopping the carnage, but rest assured that Trump will. At least that's what his speechwriter would have us believe. Trump will stop the carnage being orchestrated against the white race by the Jews.

Can we really read that intent between the lines? Why assume that anyone would hear "American carnage" that way?

There are a couple of other places where I found the word "carnage" used similarly.

In <u>White Power</u> (1966), by George Lincoln
Rockwell (founder of the American Nazi Party),
Chapter 9, "The Black Plague," you can read the
164th of 227 numbered paragraphs:

"164 Now, once again, the savage colored hordes
are terrorizing the earth, threatening to unite and
use the White Man's own fearsome technological
weapons to rape, rob, loot, plunder, murder and
enslave us in such an orgy of carnage and cruelty
as has never been dreamed of on this planet. The
Jews have let this terrible dark genie out of the
bottle to "use" him as their army in their mad
dreams of conquest of the earth, according to
their paranoiac Prophecy as the 'chosen People.'"

Another example can be found in <u>A White Man
Speaks Out</u> (1999), by Frazier Glenn Miller.

        "As a result of a half century of Jews-media
anti-White hate propaganda, the violence against

us by the colored races (and especially the Negroes) reached war-time proportions. The Negroes declared war against us, beginning in 1965, and this fact is proven by crime figures. Violent assaults against our people number in the tens of millions. And this carnage is the direct result of the Jews who sicked [sic] them on us with their hate propaganda.

Make no mistake about it, the Jews intend to exterminate the White Aryan Race from the face of the earth. Their deep down guttural hatred of everything Aryan must be understood."

In case you're not familiar with the name of Frazier Glenn Miller, he was the creator and leader of the Carolina Knights of the Ku Klux Klan, and of the White Patriot Party. Not loved by everyone in the white supremacist movement, since he testified against some of his partners in crime as part of a plea deal. Still, he has his supporters. Even after, on April 13th, 2014, he shot and killed three people at a Jewish community center and a Jewish retirement home, simply because he believed they were Jewish (they weren't).

Now, it might not look too good for our president to publicly appeal to neo-Nazis, but that was precisely what he needed to do. How else would they know, right away, that he was "/our guy/," as they call anyone who is on their side? So he had to speak in code. A code that they would recognize but that would go right over everyone else's head.

People call that kind of thing a "dog whistle." It's how racists signal each other, and they're good at it.

No, Trump isn't clever enough to figure any of that out for himself. Obviously. But Steve Bannon of *Breitbart News*, assumed to be the principal if not only speechwriter, certainly is. And on August 15, 2017, the neo-Nazi website *Occidental Dissent* proudly proclaimed, "Steve Bannon Confirmed for /Our Guy/."

Why would our president be reaching out to the ugliest fringe racist elements?

Our world is at war. There are the globalists and the anti-globalists. The anti-globalists are appealing to genocidal racists in an attempt to destabilize and break up the democratic nations of the world so that Russia can take over. "Eurasianism," or "The Eurasist Movement," are names for this Russian scheme, which is discussed in my book *Weaponized People: Trump's Eurasian Army of Trolls.*

President Trump, Steve Bannon, and the rest of Trump's crew—the entire alt-right, in fact--are all in bed with Russia. For personal gain, in some of the cases; or because some of the people genuinely believe that Russia is the best guardian of traditional values; or because Russia is willing to support ideologies incompatible with the U.S. Constitution; or in some cases, out of ignorance— merely going along with what everybody else in the Republican Party is doing.

One of the main tools used to unite haters everywhere has always been anti-Semitism.

Perhaps you may be unwilling to accept that Trump et al. are trying to signal their support for neo-Nazis in an attempt to sabotage the United States. I invite you to think of a nobler reason for them to be signaling to the Neo-Nazis. It is my contention that that's what they are doing.

But Bannon and Trump can't be anti-Semites because they're pro-Israel? It turns out that there are racists who want to send all the Jews to Israel. Just get them out of here and leave the white race alone, is the racists' thinking. Or maybe they see Israel as a more reliable ally than the Muslim states in that region. Or it could be out of respect for certain biblical prophecies.

Or perhaps their motivation is to turn Israel into one big death camp.

Whatever their sick reasoning, it seems to be true that there are some anti-Semites who support Israel.

Now, you might be saying that Trump isn't an anti-Semite because his son-in-law is Jewish. Or that this speech can't be anti-Semitic because Trump's policy advisor Stephen Miller, a Jew, was perhaps involved with writing it.

There are always Jews who will collaborate with anti-Semites for whatever reason, just as there are blacks who willingly assist white racists and women who will defend misogynists.

It may have to do with the Trump administration's support for Israel, or hatred for Muslims. Maybe agreement on other issues. Maybe perceived self-interest. Better to be with the enemy of the Jews than against them?

Yes, there are Jews who are enablers of, if not active participants in, the anti-Semitic alt-right movement. I'll name a couple of others (though by no means the only others): right-wing radio talk show hosts Mark Levin and Michael Savage, whom I used to listen to. Ridiculing diversity, and in Michael Savage's case, touting the idea of "Borders, Language, Culture" as the foundation of our country.

Those fools. Don't they realize how what they're saying will be used against them as Jews if the racists they're encouraging do succeed in getting what they want? Maybe these prominent Jews should get on the internet and see how they're referred to in the alt-right movement. They're always "Jews." And that isn't mentioned in a complimentary way. Often it's accompanied by obscenities. It doesn't matter how clever they may think they are, or how aligned with the cause. They're just "Jews." And many of the people in the ranks of the alt-right are actually Nazis of one stripe or another. Not figuratively but literally. They love Hitler.

The American Nazi Party, on its website, makes a point of saying that they welcome allies who aren't of the Aryan race but are sympathetic to the Nazi cause. They tell you that Hitler didn't just go around like a madman, killing everyone of those other races—there were people who helped him whom he spared. How moderate and rational of him.

So, we have some high-profile Jews who are willing to give aid and comfort to the Nazis. But what about when the man who just assumed the title of President of the United States himself does it?

We've already seen him do it, when during an interview he refused to condemn white supremacists and claimed not to know who David Duke was. Or when he failed to mention Jews on Holocaust Remembrance Day. Or when, most outrageously, he insisted that there were "very fine people on both sides, on both sides" of the August 2017 "Unite the Right" Nazi/KKK rally in Charlottesville NC, in which Heather Heyer, a woman protesting the rally, was killed by one of the Nazis.

So we've seen that the President is perfectly comfortable with these violent racists, willing to praise and encourage them. What most of us didn't realize at the time was that his nomination acceptance speech was one example of his doing that. He wasn't really speaking to us, he was speaking past us. (Or his speechwriter was.) And the neo-Nazis and their ilk knew exactly what he meant.

References and Sources:

Blake, Aaron. "Trump's full inauguration speech transcript, annotated." *The Washington Post.* January 20, 2017.

Capehart, Jonathan. "A petition to 'stop white genocide'?" *The Washington Post.* January 18, 2013.

Coudenhove-Kalergi, Richard von. *Praktischer Idealismus (Practical Idealism).* 1925.

Cunningham, Jalin P. and Sabate, Ignacio. "Pro-Trump E-Mail Urging Students to 'Fight White Genocide' Circulates College." *The Harvard Crimson,* October 4, 2016.

Elsis, Mark R. "Deputy Fuhrer Rudolf Hess: a Courageous Hero for Peace." August 17, 2012. (From: rudolfhess.net.)

Elsis, Mark R. "Rudolf Hess: Martyr for Peace, Murdered by Jews." May 12, 2016. (From: "Hidden in Plain Site, wordpress.com.)

Federbush, Laurel. *Weaponized People: Trump's Eurasian Army of Trolls.* 2017.

"Frazier Glenn Miller," SPLC Southern Poverty Law Center, https://www.splcenter.org/fighting-hate/extremist-files/individual/frazier-glenn-miller.

Ford, Henry. *The International Jew: The World's Foremost Problem.* 1920.

Hamilton, Andrew. "Rudolf Hess Viewed as a Member of the German Opposition." March 21, 2014. (From: Counter-Currents Publishing.)

Hitchcock, Andrew Carrington. "Jewish Genocide of the White Race – Case Closed!" March 1, 2015. (From: andrewcarringtonhitchcock.com.)

Hitler, Adolph. "Reichstag Speech." 1939. (From: N.H. Baines, editor. *The Speeches of Adolph Hitler, I.* 1942. Shoah Resource Center, The International School for Holocaust Studies.)

https://aryanoccultnation.weebly.com/jews-are-reptilian-hybrids.html

http://whitegenocideproject.com/unlike-obama-trumps-white-house-bars-petition-opposes-white-genocide/?cid=107161

Irving, David. *Hess: the Missing Years 1941-1945.* London: MacMillan London Ltd., 1987.

Lowndes, Joseph. "American Carnage." "The Blog." *Huffpost.* January 23, 2017.

Marlowe, Christopher. *The Jew of Malta.* 1589-90.

Miller, Frazier Glenn. *A White Man Speaks Out.* 1999.

Moser, Bob. "Donald Trump, Neo-Nazi Recruiter-in-Chief." *New Republic.* August 14, 2017.

"Non-Aryan Sympathizer Page." (From: http://www.americannaziparty.com/sympathizer/sympathizer.php.)

"The Nuremberg Defendants." (From: https://4rs.neocities.org/nur01.html.)

The Protocols of the Elders of Zion. "The Britons" translation. 1903.

"The Reptilian Origins of the Jews."
http://www.angelfire.com/dawn666blacksun/Reptilian.html

Rockwell, George Lincoln. *White Power.* 1966.

Sanchez, Juan O. *Religion and the Ku Klux Klan: Biblical Appropriation in Their Literature and Songs.* 2016.

Sheed, Wilfred. "The Good Word." (From: "Archives/1972.") *The New York Times.* Sept. 3, 1972.

Smith, Alistair. *Carnage: the German Front in World War One (Images of War).* Barnsley, South Yorkshire Pen & Sword. 2012.

"Steve Bannon Confirmed for /Our Guy/," *Occidental Dissent.* August 15, 2017.

Villet, Charles. "Donald Trump, White Victimhood, and the South African far-right." *The Conversation.* February 23, 2017.

Walker, Justin. *Bankers, Bradburys, Carnage and Slaughter on the Western Front.* November 2012.

whitegenocideproject.com

Wikipedia. "The Jew of Malta. Play by Christopher Marlowe."

Wikipedia. "Richard von Coudenhove-Kalergi."

Wikipedia. "Protocols of the Elders of Zion."

Thanks to Marty Shichtman for his insights.